To Uncle Al, who imagined I could be an artist

—R. G.

To Jane and Lori, who have always imagined great things for me

—S. L. T.

To learn more about Rob Gonsalves' work, or to find his work in a gallery near you,
please visit www.discoverygalleries.com or the Discovery Gallery at 4840 Bethesda Avenue,
Bethesda, Maryland 20814; (301) 913-9199.

Atheneum Books for Young Readers
An imprint of Simon & Schuster
Children's Publishing Division
1230 Avenue of the Americas
New York, New York 10020
Book design by Abelardo Martínez
The text for this book is set in Centaur and Oberon.
The illustrations for this book are rendered in acrylics.
Manufactured in China

First Edition
10 9 8 7 6 5 4 3 2 1
Library of Congress Cataloging-in-Publication Data
Gonsalves, Rob.
Imagine a day / paintings by Rob Gonsalves ;
text by Sarah L. Thomson.—1st ed.
p.   cm.
Summary: Whimsical thoughts bring colorful
and happy images to the reader.
ISBN 0-689-85219-3
[1. Imagination—Fiction.] I. Thomson, Sarah L.
II. Title.
PZ7.G5873Ik 2005
[E]—dc22   2004001033

imagine

A DAY

imagi

written by SARAH L. THOMSON

paintings by ROB GONSALVES

a byron preiss visual publications, inc. book

atheneum books for young readers

NEW YORK   LONDON   TORONTO   SYDNEY

ONE A DAY

© Gonsalves 2001

imagine a day . . .

. . . when you can dive

down through branches

or swim up

to the sun.

imagine a day . . .

. . . when grace and daring
are all we need
to build a bridge.

imagine a day . . .

. . . when your wishes float

on a puff of air

to summon back the blue.

imagine a day . . .

. . . when your house enfolds you

like a nest,

rocking gently

in the autumn wind.

imagine a day . . .

. . . when you forget

how to fall.

imagine a day . . .

. . . when we build a moat,

not to keep strangers out,

but to welcome them in.

imagine a day . . .

. . . when you don't

need wings

to soar.

imagine a day . . .

. . . when autumn is

a yellow canopy above you,

a burnt orange carpet underneath,

a road you have never

ridden on before.

imagine a day . . .

. . . when everything you build

touches the sky.

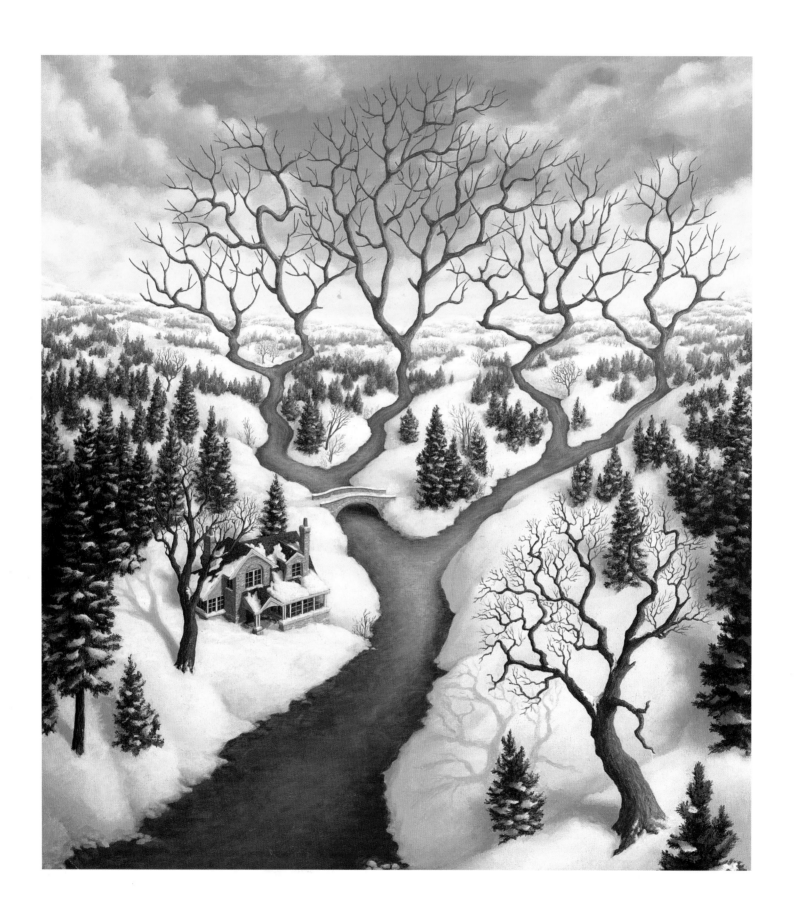

imagine a day . . .

. . . when roots drink up rivers,

twigs tangle in clouds,

and a tree is a ladder

between earth and air.

imagine a day . . .

. . . when you build the world

around you

piece by piece.

imagine a day . . .

. . . when the edge of the map

is only the beginning

of what we can explore.

imagine a day . . .

. . . when your sand castle

can withstand

even the highest waves.

imagine a day . . .

. . . when the peace of a forest

and the strength of a mountain

become a cathedral

for your heart.

imagine a day . . .

. . . when a book swings open

on silent hinges,

and a place you've never seen before

welcomes you home.

Imagine . . . today.